FIGURATIVE LANGUAG

Table of Contents

Introduction 1
Assessment 3

Unit 1: Concepts
Literal and Figurative Language 5
Analogies 7
Similes 13
Poetry Devices 15
Homographs 17
Homophones 18

Unit 2: Applications
Using Literal and Figurative Language 19
Finding Similes 21
Writing Poems 24
Using Homographs 25
Using Homophones 26

Unit 3: Enrichment
Homograph Riddles 27
Finding Homophones 28
Fun with Homographs and Homophones 29
Jokes 30
Poetry Fun 31

Answer Key 33

Introduction

Most of the elementary curriculum today is aimed at literal education—adding numbers, remembering facts. Little of the curriculum deals with critical thinking: interpreting, analyzing, using abstract or figurative language. This book, *Figurative Language*, attempts to promote practice in critical thinking. The students must learn to recognize figurative devices that yield a secondary level of meaning.

A variety of lessons and activities gives students practice in literal and figurative thought. They make literal comparisons to learn logical relationships. Then, they move on to figurative comparisons, in which the relationships are more abstract. The students are also exposed to poetic devices. Finally, the students study homographs and homophones, seeing that words can be fun to work with.

This book is divided into three units.

- Unit 1 covers the concepts of literal and figurative language, with particular emphasis on analogies, similes, and metaphors.

- Unit 2 covers the application of those concepts, as students distinguish between literal and figurative language and identify figurative devices.

- Unit 3 provides enrichment activities, in which the students use language to solve riddles and make jokes. All the units stress a higher level of thought and provide many writing activities.

At the first of the book is a general assessment. It can be used before the students begin the activities to determine a benchmark. The assessment can then be used after the activities have been completed to gauge students' progress. At the end of many activities is a

"More to Do" section. This section invites the students to use the concepts they have learned to create their own works.

As a final note, be aware that there are several instances of misused words in this book, especially in Unit 3. These misused words are meant to demonstrate the playful nature of language.

Teaching Figurative Language

Literal comparisons, which are often called analogies, provide the students with a form of critical thinking. They must recognize the important relationship between the part and the whole, and they must also recognize the relationships between sets of objects. This book provides practice in making literal comparisons.

The most important aspect of teaching figurative language is enabling the students to see that the author is saying two things at once. One of the levels is always literal.

The man ran across the street.

This example uses nouns, verbs, and prepositions to describe an action literally. The second level of meaning is figurative.

The man ran across the street <u>like a frightened cat.</u>

The simile in the second example gives the reader two images to consider, and a comparison is made between the two. One is like the other. Ask the students if they have ever seen a frightened cat move. If they have, they know more about how the man ran across the street. The students' understanding of the figurative example depends on their level of experience. Figurative devices, therefore, require the input of the reader, unlike the multiplication tables, which are a matter of rote.

Unlike in literal comparisons, though, in most figures of speech (similes, etc.), only one of the elements is literal, or concrete. The other element is usually figurative, or abstract. In figurative devices, authors often compare a more unknown quality or value (abstract) to a common thing (concrete). Robert Burns wrote long ago, "My love is like a red, red rose." If the students understand the qualities of a rose, they can enhance their understanding of love. So always point the students to the comparison being made, to the terms being compared, and to their own feelings about what the comparison means.

Figurative language, of course, is a hard subject to grade quantitatively. An assessment is included in this book, but it only gauges the more basic aspects of figurative language. Students must identify a simile or complete a comparison. The true thrust of teaching (and assessing) figurative language should be qualitative. Have the students discuss and write figurative language. The minds of young students are like undiscovered treasure mines.

Name _____ Date _____

Assessment

DIRECTIONS Read the following sentences. Decide if each sentence uses literal or figurative language. Write <u>literal</u> or <u>figurative</u> on the line.

_____ 1. The cow walked slowly along the road.

_____ 2. The backpack had many books in it.

_____ 3. The backpack was as heavy as an elephant.

_____ 4. The dog ran like the wind across the playground.

_____ 5. The volcano erupted in the dark night.

_____ 6. She was as pretty as a picture.

DIRECTIONS Choose words from the WORD BOX to complete the analogies. Not all the words in the box will be used.

WORD BOX

| hot | orange | small | nests | track |
| smell | dark | ear | caboose | chicken |

7. <u>Milk</u> is to <u>cow</u> AS <u>egg</u> is to _____.

8. <u>Houses</u> are to <u>people</u> AS _____ are to <u>birds</u>.

9. <u>Peel</u> is to _____ AS <u>skin</u> is to <u>apple</u>.

10. <u>Day</u> is to <u>night</u> AS _____ is to <u>cold</u>.

Go on to the next page.

Name _____ Date _____

Assessment, p. 2

DIRECTIONS Circle the letter of the homograph whose meaning fits both sentences.

11. I _____ a great program last night.
    You need a _____ to cut that board.
    a. heard
    b. scissors
    c. saw
    d. attended

12. That table is so _____ that it's easy to lift.
    Please turn on the _____.
    a. radio
    b. beautiful
    c. narrow
    d. light

DIRECTIONS Circle the correct homophone in ( ) to complete each sentence.

13. The store was easy to _____. (find, fined)

14. His heart _____ faster. (beet, beat)

15. At the end of the _____, Bob made a plan. (weak, week)

16. From the hilltop, Meg could _____ her house. (see, sea)

DIRECTIONS Underline the similes in the following excerpt from "A Visit from St. Nicholas," by Clement Moore.

His eyes—how they twinkled; his dimples, how merry!
His cheeks were like roses, his nose like a cherry!
His droll little mouth was drawn up like a bow,
And the beard of his chin was as white as the snow;
The stump of a pipe he held tight in his teeth,
And the smoke it encircled his head like a wreath;
He had a broad face and a little round belly
That shook, when he laughed, like a bowl full of jelly.

Name _____ Date _____

Say What You Mean!

Language helps us to communicate. With language, we can write and read. We can talk and sing. We can think and imagine. But language can be confusing, too. Some words are hard to say. Some words are hard to spell. Some words are spelled alike but mean different things. Some words sound alike but are spelled differently.

There are different kinds of language, too. Some words are **literal language**. With literal language, you say just what you mean. Literal words have an exact meaning. They let the reader see a clear mental picture, or **image**. Car is a literal word. You can see a clear picture of a car in your mind.

Another kind of language is **figurative language**. Figurative language uses exaggeration. It has a meaning not exactly like the words used. Figurative language tries to create a clear image, too. The image helps you to understand the writing better. For example, Mother Nature is figurative language. Nature is shown as a caring, helpful mother.

DIRECTIONS | **Read the three passages below. Two use figurative language. One uses literal language. Circle the two passages that use <u>figurative language</u>.**

Paul Bunyan was huge. He was so huge that he used a tree limb to comb his hair. He used a broom to brush his teeth.

There are many tall tales about Paul Bunyan. These tall tales exaggerate the things Paul does. They make Paul seem bigger and better than he really is. The tall tales are fun to hear and think about.

The gentle breeze whispered good morning to the new day. All the flowers opened their happy petals. The rising Sun said hello to the world.

REMEMBER: Literal language means what it says. Figurative language tries to give a picture of what is happening.

Go on to the next page.

Unit One: Concepts
© Steck-Vaughn Company   5   Figurative Language 3, SV 2717-0

Name _____ Date _____

Say What You Mean!, p. 2

DIRECTIONS Read the following sentences. Underline the sentence if it uses **figurative language**. Circle the sentence if it uses **literal language**.

1. Jonathan loves to play with his action figures.
2. Wally was as busy as a beaver.
3. His feet smelled like dead fish.
4. Whales can grow to over 40 feet long.
5. Paul Bunyan was as big as a tree.
6. My mother and I go to the library every Saturday.
7. That movie scared me out of my skin.
8. I found my way home without any trouble.
9. The building was very tall.
10. The building was so tall that it touched the sky.

MORE TO DO

Write one sentence that uses literal language. Write another sentence that uses figurative language.

_____
_____
_____
_____
_____

Comparisons

A comparison shows how things are alike. A comparison shows you how things are related. One kind of comparison is called an **analogy**. An analogy is a way to compare word meanings. An analogy has two parts. The two parts are joined with the word as. As means "in the same way."

<u>Hat</u> is to <u>head</u> **AS** <u>shoe</u> is to ?

To Solve an Analogy:
1. Think about how the terms in the first part are related.

    "A hat is worn on the head."

2. Then, think how this relationship works in the second part.

    "Where is a shoe worn?"

A shoe is worn on the foot. So, <u>hat</u> is to <u>head</u> **AS** <u>shoe</u> is to <u>foot</u>.

DIRECTIONS ‖‖‖ **Draw a line to the picture that correctly completes the sentence.**

1.  is to  **AS** is to _____ .

2.  is to **AS** is to _____ .

3. _____ is to _____ **AS** _____ is to _____ .

Unit One: Concepts

Name _____   Date _____

Parts of a Whole

Some analogies compare parts of a thing to the whole thing. To figure out the analogy, look for clues in the first part.

Toe is to foot AS finger is to ?

Remember, to Solve an Analogy:

1. Think about how the terms in the first part are related.

    "A toe is part of a foot."

2. Then, think how this relationship works in the second part.

    "What is a finger a part of?"

A finger is part of a hand. So, toe is to foot AS finger is to hand.

DIRECTIONS — **Circle the picture that completes each analogy.**

1. Wood is to 🏠 AS twigs are to _____ . ⛺ 🪺

2. Steering wheel is to 🚗 AS handlebars are to _____ . 🚲 🚣

3. Scales are to 🐟 AS feathers are to _____ . 🐦 🐕

4. Keys are to 🎹 AS strings are to _____ . 🎺 🎸

5. Antlers are to 🦌 AS tusks are to _____ . 🐻 🐘

✏️ **MORE TO DO** ✏️

Write your own analogies that show a relationship of a part to the whole. Try to write at least three analogies. Draw a picture to complete each analogy. Share your analogies with your classmates.

Name _____ Date _____

What About It?

Some analogies compare characteristics. They tell what things are like. Remember, to figure out the analogy, look for clues in the first part. Think about how the terms in the first part are related. Then, think how this relationship works in the second part.

DIRECTIONS | Circle the picture that completes each analogy.

1. Square is to box AS round is to _____.

2. Glass is to window AS cloth is to _____.

3. Happy is to smile AS sad is to _____.

4. Cold is to ice cream AS hot is to _____.

5. Huge is to elephant AS tiny is to _____.

6. Purple is to grapes AS red is to _____.

7. Moo is to cow AS bark is to _____.

8. White is to milk AS yellow is to _____.

MORE TO DO

Write your own analogies about characteristics. Try to write at least three analogies. Draw pictures to complete each analogy. See if your classmates can solve your analogies.

Name _____ Date _____

Keep It Moving!

Some analogies compare actions. Remember, to figure out the analogy, look for clues in the first part. Think about how the terms in the first part are related. Then, think how this relationship works in the second part.

<u>Bark</u> is to <u>dog</u> **AS** <u>meow</u> is to ?

A dog barks with its mouth. What makes the "meow" sound with its mouth?

DIRECTIONS |||| **Circle the word that completes each analogy.**

1. <u>Bird</u> is to <u>fly</u> **AS** <u>frog</u> is to _____.	run	drive	hop
2. <u>Nose</u> is to <u>smell</u> **AS** <u>eye</u> is to _____.	hear	see	feel
3. <u>Bite</u> is to <u>snake</u> **AS** <u>sting</u> is to _____.	dog	fire	bee
4. <u>Pool</u> is to <u>swim</u> **AS** <u>track</u> is to _____.	run	fly	roll
5. <u>Red</u> is to <u>stop</u> **AS** <u>green</u> is to _____.	cow	go	hop
6. <u>Throw</u> is to <u>hand</u> **AS** <u>kick</u> is to _____.	arm	head	foot
7. <u>Moo</u> is to <u>cow</u> **AS** <u>quack</u> is to _____.	cat	duck	monkey
8. <u>Pencil</u> is to <u>draw</u> **AS** <u>brush</u> is to _____.	paint	write	read
9. <u>Sniff</u> is to <u>nose</u> **AS** <u>wink</u> is to _____.	ear	eye	mouth
10. <u>Driver</u> is to <u>bus</u> **AS** <u>pilot</u> is to _____.	car	bike	airplane

✏️ **MORE TO DO** ✏️

Write your own analogies that compare actions. Try to write at least three analogies. Share your analogies with your classmates. See if they can figure out your analogies.

Opposites

Some analogies compare opposites. Remember, to figure out the analogy, look for clues in the first part. Think about how the terms in the first part are related. Then, think how this relationship works in the second part.

Sometimes, a word in the first part of the analogy is missing. Then, you have to look for clues in the second part.

Sun is to _____ AS Moon is to night.

The Moon shines at night. When does the Sun shine?

DIRECTIONS Choose words from the WORD BOX to complete these analogies. Not all the words in the box will be used.

WORD BOX

| near | thin | big | warm | right | cold | sad | dry | down | night | in | funny |

1. Hard is to soft AS wet is to _____.
2. Over is to under AS _____ is to far.
3. Hot is to _____ AS fire is to ice.
4. Day is to _____ AS light is to dark.
5. Tall is to short AS thick is to _____.
6. Small is to _____ AS loud is to quiet.
7. Left is to right AS _____ is to wrong.
8. Sharp is to dull AS happy is to _____.
9. Hot is to cold AS _____ is to cool.
10. Up is to _____ AS _____ is to out.

Name _____ Date _____

Finish It Up

DIRECTIONS | Write the word that correctly finishes the analogy.

1. Letters are to alphabet AS pages are to _____.
2. Mother is to father AS aunt is to _____.
3. Milk is to cow AS egg is to _____.
4. Blood is to person AS sap is to _____.
5. Fly is to bird AS swim is to _____.

DIRECTIONS | Draw a line to connect the first part of the analogy to the second part.

AS

6. Dog is to puppy   a. woman is to mother.

7. Plumber is to pipes   b. cat is to kitten.

8. Summer is to rain   c. fangs are to snake.

9. Man is to father   d. dentist is to teeth.

10. Teeth are to dog   e. winter is to snow.

© Steck-Vaughn Company

12

Unit One: Concepts
Figurative Language 3, SV 2717-0

Similes

Similes are another kind of comparison. Similes use figurative language. The writer compares two things that are not really alike. What two things are compared in the following sentence?

The girl ran from the bees like a frightened cat.

If you said that the running girl and the frightened cat are being compared, you are right! The sentence gives you two ideas to think about. Have you ever seen a frightened cat move? If you have, you have a better idea about how the girl ran. The clue word like is used to make this comparison. When like or as is used to compare two things, the comparison is called a **simile**.

DIRECTIONS In each sentence below, underline the two things being compared.

1. His smile was like sunshine.
2. She was as quiet as a mouse.
3. Sheila acted like a monster.
4. He was busy as a beaver.
5. My brother acts like a clown.
6. The rain sounded like rocks hitting the roof.
7. The crowd roared like thunder.
8. The kitten was as snug as a bug in a rug.

Name _____ Date _____

It's as Easy as Pie

To Recognize Similes:
1. **READ** the sentence carefully.
2. **THINK** what things are being compared.
3. **LOOK** for the use of <u>like</u> or <u>as</u> to signal a simile.

DIRECTIONS **Read each comparison. Underline the <u>simile</u>. Then, tell which two things are being compared.**

1. The dogs ran like the wind across the playground.
   _____

2. My life is sometimes like a circus.
   _____

3. The thick grass was like carpet under our feet.
   _____

4. She was as funny as a monkey.
   _____

5. The room was as hot as an oven.
   _____

6. The Moon was like a silver ship sailing through a cloudy sea.
   _____

Name _____ Date _____

Rhyme Time

Words that end with the same sounds are **rhyming words**. Here are some rhyming words.

car—star   boat—goat   top—drop

A **rhyme** is two or more lines that end with rhyming words. Many rhymes are silly or funny.

Fred Frog rode a rocket to the moon.
He left in July and came back in June.

How to Write a Rhyme:
1. **WRITE** two lines.
2. **END** each line with a rhyming word.

DIRECTIONS | **Finish each rhyme. Add rhyming words. You may use words from the WORD BOX.**

WORD BOX

| cow | dog | bee | hat |

1. Did you ever see a cat

   Wear a funny _____?

2. The cat climbed down a tree

   And sang a song with a

   _____.

3. The bee said, "meow,"

   And flew off to visit the

   _____.

4. The cow watched Fred Frog

   Hop over a _____.

Name _____ Date _____

Word Art

In a **poem** a writer paints a picture with words. Poems often describe things in an unusual or interesting way. Poems use figurative language. Many poems also have **rhyming words**. The words in a poem often have a **rhythm**, or **beat**.

Star light, star bright,
First star I see tonight,
I wish I may, I wish I might,
Have this wish I wish tonight.

How to Write a Poem:
1. **CHOOSE** a topic for your poem.
2. **THINK** of colorful words to paint a picture.
3. **USE** rhyme and rhythm to show your feelings.
4. **THEN** give your poem a title.

DIRECTIONS **Finish the poem. Think of colorful words and words that rhyme. Write another verse for the poem. Then, think of a title for your poem.**

_____

Fred Frog wants a drink.

He hops in the sink.

The _____ water comes down.

Will Fred Frog frown?

_____
_____
_____

At Home with Homographs

Homographs are words that are spelled the same but that have different meanings. The words may also be pronounced differently. <u>Tear</u>, meaning "to rip," and <u>tear</u>, meaning "a water drop from the eye," are homographs.

She filled the <u>pitcher</u> with lemonade.
The <u>pitcher</u> threw the ball to the catcher.

My mother likes to play the card game of <u>bridge</u>.
The cars drove across the <u>bridge</u>.

DIRECTIONS **Circle the letter of the homograph with the meaning that fits both sentences.**

1. I _____ come with you this afternoon.
   Open the _____ of food for the dog.
   a. will
   b. should
   c. bag
   d. can

2. Use a key to _____ the door.
   She saved a _____ of the baby's hair.
   a. curl
   b. lock
   c. open
   d. piece

3. Manny is a big hockey _____.
   Turn on the _____! It's hot in here.
   a. fan
   b. radio
   c. player
   d. light

4. Fill the cereal _____ with milk.
   Did you ever _____ on Jeri's team?
   a. jar
   b. bowl
   c. swim
   d. dish

Answer the Homophone!

Homophones are words that sound the same but are spelled differently. They also have different meanings. <u>To</u>, <u>too</u>, and <u>two</u> are homophones. Be careful with homophones. If you write the wrong homophone, you may not be saying what you mean. Is this sentence correct?

Wood you like to sea a movie?

DIRECTIONS | **Complete each sentence correctly. Choose the correct homophone in ( ), and write it in the blank.**

1. They had heard the strange noise _____ times.
   (to, too, two)

2. I planted a _____ in my garden.
   (flour, flower)

3. The movie lasted one _____.
   (our, hour)

4. The man _____ his horse down the _____.
   (road, rode)

5. Can you untie the _____ in the rope?
   (not, knot)

6. Do you _____ the _____ home?
   (no, know; way, weigh)

DIRECTIONS | **Think of a homophone for each of these words. Write it on the line next to the word.**

7. here _____   8. their _____

9. ate _____   10. for _____

Name _____ Date _____

It Was How Big?

Read these two sentences. Think about what they mean.

The boy's smile was as wide as the ocean.
The boy had a big smile on his face.

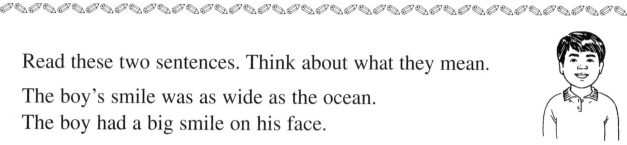

How are these two sentences alike? Yes, they are both talking about a boy's big smile. How are they different? The first one uses **figurative language**. Could the boy's smile be as wide as the ocean? Of course not. The author has exaggerated how big the boy's smile is. This kind of writing makes the sentence more interesting.

The second sentence uses **literal language**. The sentence means just what it says. The first one doesn't literally mean what it says.

To Tell the Difference Between Figurative and Literal Language:
1. **READ** the sentence carefully.
2. **THINK** about the meaning of the sentence.
3. **DECIDE** if the sentence means just what it says (literal), or if it has exaggerated what it means (figurative).

DIRECTIONS Read the following sentences. Decide if they are using figurative or literal language. Write <u>literal</u> or <u>figurative</u> on the line.

_____ **1.** The woman had a long neck.

_____ **2.** The woman's neck was as long as a giraffe's.

_____ **3.** David ate a ton of food for lunch.

_____ **4.** David ate a big lunch.

_____ **5.** Tina is a monster when she gets mad.

_____ **6.** Tina is hard to get along with when she gets mad.

Name _____ Date _____

But What You Really Mean Is

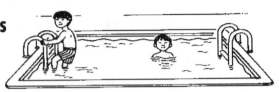

DIRECTIONS Each sentence below uses figurative language. Write a literal sentence to tell what each sentence really means.

1. Karen was beginning to melt from the heat.
   _____

2. I jumped out of my skin when Doug scared me.
   _____

3. John had been in the pool for weeks.
   _____

4. Ella turns into a fish when she gets into the water.
   _____

5. Ted was up to his neck in work.
   _____

6. When Mike talks, you can hear him a mile away.
   _____

7. Mother carries everything but the kitchen sink in her purse.
   _____

8. As the plane went higher, the people on the ground turned into ants.
   _____

Name _____ Date _____

Finding Similes

Figurative language uses **figures of speech**. One figure of speech is the **simile**. A simile compares two things that are not really alike. For example, a simile would be, "The boy ran <u>like</u> a flash of lightning." The simile compares the boy's running to a flash of lightning.

Similes use the words <u>like</u> or <u>as</u> to show the comparison. But be careful. Not all sentences that have the word <u>like</u> contain a simile. For example, "I do not <u>like</u> cats" is not a simile.

DIRECTIONS — **Underline the similes in the following poem.**

Little Fred Frog is a funny guy.
Sometimes he buzzes like a fly.
Sometimes he meows like a hungry cat.
Sometimes he squeaks like a lonely rat.
But yesterday, asleep in his house,
Fred Frog was as quiet as a mouse.

DIRECTIONS — **Complete the following similes.**

1. The boy laughed like _____.
2. He was as funny as _____.
3. She was as pretty as _____.
4. The dog was as friendly as _____.

✏️ **MORE TO DO** ✏️

With a partner, write five similes. Make up the first part of the simile. For example, you might write, "The wet cat smelled like _____." Then, both of you should fill in the last part of the simile. Draw a picture to go with each simile. When you are finished, share your similes with your classmates.

Name _____   Date _____

More Similes

DIRECTIONS |||| Read each sentence. Underline the two things that are being compared. Then, tell how they are alike.

1. The fog comes in like a cat.
   _____

2. The fog covered the hill like a blanket.
   _____

3. The tree, like an umbrella, protected us from the rain.
   _____

4. The grasshoppers called back and forth like an echo.
   _____

5. The Moon smiled down on us, just as Grandma always did.
   _____

6. Like a mirror, the lake reflected the light.
   _____

7. Like a knife through butter, the boat slipped through the water.
   _____

✎✐ MORE TO DO ✎✐

Write your own sentences that use similes. See if your classmates can find your similes.

Unit Two: Applications

Name _____ Date _____

Using Similes

Good writers create vivid word pictures. They compare two things that are not really alike. These comparisons are called **similes**.

DIRECTIONS | **Read the paragraph. Then, complete the sentences.**

The deep lake was like a golden mirror reflecting the setting Sun. Like a large ball of orange wax slowly melting, the Sun slipped below the treetops. Across the water, a row of mountain peaks looked like jagged teeth. Beyond the mountains, the sunset blazed like a pink and orange flame.

1. One simile compares _____ to _____.

2. Another simile compares _____ to _____.

3. The third simile compares _____ to _____.

4. The last simile compares _____ to _____.

DIRECTIONS | **Complete each simile.**

5. The white clouds were like _____.

6. The warm breeze was like _____.

7. The rows of corn were like _____.

8. The falling autumn leaves were like _____.

Unit Two: Applications

Name _____ Date _____

Write a Poem

In a poem, a poet paints a picture or expresses a feeling with words. The poet may use similes to write the poem. The poet often uses rhythm and rhyme in the poem. The poet may also use **alliteration**. This means using many words that begin with the same sound. Many tongue-twisters use alliteration.

The dark duck dropped into the dirty drainpipe. Here, the "d" sound is repeated.

Halloween
Goblins and witches in the night
Give everyone a terrible fright.
Creepy creaks on every stair,
Bats dark as night fly everywhere.
Many strange costumes to be seen—
Hooray, it's Halloween!

How to Write a Poem:
1. **CHOOSE** a topic for your poem.
2. **THINK** of colorful words to paint a picture for your audience.
3. **USE** rhyme and rhythm to express feeling.
4. **USE** words that begin with the same sound.
5. **MAKE** comparisons between two things that do not seem alike.
6. **THEN** give your poem a title.

DIRECTIONS Finish this poem. Add colorful words that rhyme, compare, or add sound. Then, give the poem a title.

_____

A jack-o-lantern's _____ smile

Glowed like a _____ in the

_____ night,

Till an owl flew _____ with a

_____ cry

And the _____ wind blew out the

_____ .

Unit Two: Applications
Figurative Language 3, SV 2717-0

Name _____ Date _____

Alike and Different

Homographs are words that have the same spelling but different meanings.

felt—a soft kind of cloth
felt—sensed something on the skin

Some homographs are pronounced differently.

wind—moving air
wind—to turn a knob on something, such as a clock

DIRECTIONS Write a new sentence with the homograph of the underlined word. Be sure to use a different meaning of the underlined word in your sentence. Use a dictionary if you need help.

1. Manny found a baseball <u>bat</u> on the beach. _____
_____

2. Mari looked at the tree <u>bark</u>. _____
_____

3. Was there a <u>tear</u> on Teri's face? _____
_____

4. <u>Can</u> you think of all the words? _____
_____

5. The cook poured the cake <u>batter</u> into the pan. _____
_____

Name _____ Date _____

Can You See the Sea?

Homophones are words that sound alike. They are spelled differently and have different meanings.

Beth did the <u>right</u> thing.
Did she <u>write</u> a thank-you note?

"Please <u>be</u> my friend!" Beth begged.
Beth ran away from the <u>bee</u>.

DIRECTIONS | **Complete each sentence correctly. Choose the correct homophone in ( ), and write it in the blank.**

1. The girl _____ the sign that told about the puppies.
   (red, read)

2. _____ the man sell her a puppy?
   (Would, Wood)

3. A _____ of puppies were lying in the grass.
   (pear, pair)

4. The girl thought she could _____ her mother.
   (here, hear)

5. The puppy wagged his _____ .
   (tail, tale)

MORE TO DO

Write five sentence like the ones above. Leave a blank in each sentence, and have answer choices at the end. Then, let a classmate try to complete your sentences.

Name _____ Date _____

Home on the Range

Homographs are words that have the same spelling but different meanings. Sometimes homographs have different pronunciations.

We <u>park</u> our car in the <u>park</u>.

<u>Live</u> animals are not allowed in the building where we <u>live</u>.

DIRECTIONS Read each riddle. Tell what the underlined word means in each riddle. Then, write a sentence to show a different meaning for each underlined word.

1. Question: When is a piece of wood like a king?
   Answer: when it's a <u>ruler</u>

   Meaning: _____

   Your sentence: _____
   _____

2. Question: Why do watermelons have water in them?
   Answer: because they are planted in the <u>spring</u>
   Meaning: _____

   Your sentence: _____
   _____

3. Question: Why did the farmer call his pig Ink?
   Answer: because it always kept running out of the <u>pen</u>
   Meaning: _____

   Your sentence: _____
   _____

✎✎ MOOR TWO DEW ✎✎

Make up your own riddles using homographs. Share your riddles with your classmates. Can they answer the riddles?

Unit Three: Enrichment

Name _____   Date _____

Wears the Homophone?

Homophones are words that sound the same but are spelled differently. They also have different meanings. <u>Blue</u> and <u>blew</u> are homophones. If you write the wrong homophone, you may not be saying what you really mean.

DIRECTIONS | **Read each sentence below. Find each homophone that is used incorrectly. Underline it. Then, rewrite the sentences using the correct words.**

1. Do you no how to go to the library?
   _____

2. No won is aloud to talk during a fire drill.
   _____

3. Wee are studying sells in hour science class.
   _____

4. Cecile red a book of tall tails.
   _____

5. The night wore a knew suit of armor.
   _____

6. When I am board, I right poems.
   _____

✎ MOOR TWO DEW ✎

Write five sentences that use homophones incorrectly. Let a classmate find the homophones. Then, the classmate should rewrite your sentences using the correct words. For extra fun, draw a picture that illustrates one of the incorrect sentences.

Have You Herd the Gnus?

Some words are spelled and written the same way, but they mean different things. These words are called **homographs**. <u>Homo</u> means "same," and <u>graph</u> means "write." <u>Ball</u>, meaning "a game toy," and <u>ball</u>, meaning "a fancy dance," are homographs.

Some words sound alike, but they are spelled differently. They also mean different things. These words are called **homophones**. <u>Phone</u> means "sound." <u>Sun</u> and <u>son</u> are homophones.

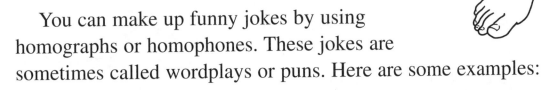

You can make up funny jokes by using homographs or homophones. These jokes are sometimes called wordplays or puns. Here are some examples:

Yesterday, my nose was running . . . down the street!

I taught my dog to heel . . . and now he's a doctor in Roverville!

DIRECTIONS — Underline the <u>homograph</u> or <u>homophone</u> in each sentence.

1. Did you ever hear Aesop's fable of the tortoise and the hair?
2. How do you know the ocean is friendly? Because it waves.
3. Why do we sit in the stands at the ball game?
4. What did the hat say to the hat rack? You stay here; I'll go on ahead.
5. Seven days in bed makes one weak.

✎✎ MOOR TWO DEW ✎✎

Write your own funny lines using homophones and homographs. Underline the word or group of words that makes the wordplay.

Name _____   Date _____

Jokes

Many jokes use homographs and homophones. The wordplays can be very funny. See how this joke uses a homophone.

Question: If you were lost in a desert, how could you survive?
Answer: You could eat the sand which is (sandwiches) there.

DIRECTIONS | **Here are some more jokes. Share them with your friends.**

1. Why did Fred Frog take a ruler to bed?
   (To see how long he slept)

2. What kind of dog is best able to keep time?
   (A watch dog)

3. Why did the chicken cross the playground?
   (To get to the other slide)

4. When is a car not a car?
   (When it turns into a driveway)

5. What did the baby corn call its father?
   (Pop Corn)

6. What do you call a butcher's dance?
   (A meatball)

7. What kind of wood should you use to build a cow shed?
   (Cattle logs)

8. What gets bigger <u>and</u> smaller the more you take away from it?
   (A hole/whole)

MOOR TWO DEW

Make up your own jokes using homographs and homophones. Tell your jokes to your classmates. Have a contest to see who has the funniest jokes.

Name _____ Date _____

Write a Cloud Poem

Have you ever watched clouds? They change shape often. Look up at the clouds. Watch them go by. What do they make you think of?

Example: Clouds look like camels running across the sky.

DIRECTIONS | **List what things or animals the clouds make you think about. Then, write a poem about cloud shapes.**

✏️ MOOR TWO DEW ✏️

Look at the sky at sunset. What do you think about? Write a poem about sunset.

Unit Three: Enrichment
Figurative Language 3, SV 2717-0
© Steck-Vaughn Company

Name _____   Date _____

Poetry Fun

Now you know all about figurative language and poems. So you are ready to write some good poems. Think carefully about the words you use in your poems. Try to use all the poet's tools to make your poem better.

DIRECTIONS | **Use the activities below to help you write.**

1. With a partner, find a picture of a pretty scene in a magazine. Each of you should write five similes that describe the picture. Choose the six best similes or metaphors. Cut out the picture, and paste it at the top of a piece of paper. Under the picture, use the six best similes to write a poem about the picture.

2. Write a song that has rhyming words. Sing the song for your class.

3. Use alliteration to write a tongue-twister poem. Here's an example:

   Peter Piper picked a peck of pickled peppers.
   A peck of pickled peppers Peter Piper picked.
   If Peter Piper picked a peck of pickled peppers,
   Where's the peck of pickled peppers Peter Piper picked?

4. With a partner, write a poem that rhymes. Make up five sets of rhymes. If you can't think of any rhymes, try these: blue/new; bed/bread; go/snow; bright/white; dog/log. You should choose one of the words in each set. Your partner gets the other word in each set. Then, each of you should write lines for your poem that end with the rhyming words. Finally, write out the poem, using the lines written by both partners. Arrange the lines any way you like. You have poetic license!